# TAKE TEN YEARS

# 1980s

Evans

EVANS BROTHERS LIMITED

# Contents

The pictures on page 4 show
Royal wedding – the Prince and Princess of Wales
Falklands crisis – the Royal Navy Task Force
Famine refugees in camp in Ethiopia
Live Aid concert, London

The pictures on page 5 show
Mikhail Gorbachev
Russian troops leaving Afghanistan
George Bush during election campaign
Tian-an-men Square, Beijing, China
San Francisco earthquake
Dismantling the Berlin Wall

# Introduction

The Eighties was a decade of political violence, much as the Seventies had been. Three major conflicts dragged on for nearly the whole ten years. Iran and Iraq fought each other to a standstill. Thousands died, but in the end, neither side could claim a victory. In Afghanistan, the mujahaddin fought a long and lonely war against the Russian invaders. On the shores of the Mediterranean, Lebanon was torn apart by internal strife and foreign invasion. Smaller wars, such as the one fought over the Falkland Islands, also made the headlines. There were a series of assassination attempts, some of them fatal. All over the world, there was pressure for change.

At the beginning of the Eighties, the main new power was militant Islam. In Tehran, the Ayatollah Khomeini preached Islamic fundamentalism, imposing strict traditional values on Iranian society. His teachings appealed to poor people in many Muslim countries.

Russia was still a superpower, but began to feel the need for political change. The Afghan war was unpopular, and the shops were empty of the things people wanted to buy. There was an urgent need for reform. A strong leader emerged. Mikhail Gorbachev announced new policies of *glasnost* (openness) and *perestroika* (reconstruction).

By the late Eighties, there was similar unrest throughout the Communist countries of Eastern Europe. The leader of this movement was the Polish trade union, Solidarity. For most of the Eighties, Solidarity was a lone voice calling for democracy. By the end of the decade, a wave of reform was sweeping across Eastern Europe.

Democracy also spread to other parts of the globe. In China, it flourished very briefly, before being crushed by the authorities. In the Philippines, a dictator was overthrown, and a democratic government was formed.

In the developed world, the Eighties was generally a decade of prosperity, despite a disastrous stock market crash. Yet it was also a time of concern, both for the suffering of other people and for the future of the planet as a whole. Through charity events such as the music industry's Band Aid and Live Aid, young people raised large amounts of money for famine relief in Africa.

| YEARS | WORLD AFFAIRS |
|-------|---------------|
| **1980** | US hostage rescue attempt fails<br>SAS rescue hostages in Iranian embassy<br>Mr. Mugabe becomes Zimbabwe's Prime Minister |
| **1981** | American hostages in Iran released<br>Martial law declared in Poland<br>Belize gains independence from Britain |
| **1982** | PLO evicted from Lebanon by Israelis<br>Massacre of Palestinian refugees<br>Socialists win power in Spain<br>Solidarity trade union banned in Poland |
| **1983** | Syrians evict PLO from Lebanon<br>OPEC cuts world price of oil |
| **1984** | |
| **1985** | Mikhail Gorbachev comes to power in USSR<br>Anglo-Irish Agreement signed<br>AIDS declared an epidemic |
| **1986** | President Marcos of Philippines is ousted<br>'Irangate' scandal in America |
| **1987** | Mr. Gorbachev announces reforms in USSR<br>Fiji gains independence |
| **1988** | Independence gained for Namibia<br>PLO recognize state of Israel |
| **1989** | Berlin Wall opened<br>Solidarity wins elections in Poland<br>Hungary opens its border with Austria |

| WARS & CIVIL DISORDER | PEOPLE | EVENTS |
|---|---|---|
| War between Iran and Iraq | Lech Walesa leads Solidarity<br>Ronald Reagan becomes US President<br>Peter Sellers, actor, dies<br>Ex-Beatle John Lennon shot dead | Volcano erupts in USA<br>USA boycotts Olympic Games in Moscow |
| Coup attempt in Spain fails<br>Riots in British cities | Assassination of President Sadat of Egypt<br>François Mitterrand elected President of France<br>Bob Marley, reggae singer, dies | New party, SDP, launched in Britain<br>Doctors identify new disease, AIDS<br>Space shuttle launched in USA<br>Prince Charles marries Lady Diana Spencer |
| War in Falkland Islands | Leonid Brezhnev of USSR dies<br>Moonie leader jailed | *Mary Rose* wreck raised from sea bed<br>European court bans cane in schools<br>Women's peace camp established at US air base in UK |
| Islamic fundamentalists bomb troops in Beirut<br>USA invades Grenada | Margaret Thatcher re-elected in Britain<br>Benigno Aquino murdered in Philippines<br>Lech Walesa wins Nobel Peace Prize | Russia shoots down Korean airliner<br>USA announces 'Star Wars' defence system<br>Australia wins America's Cup |
| IRA bomb Conservatives at party conference | Indira Gandhi assassinated<br>Polish priest killed for supporting Solidarity<br>Ronald Reagan re-elected US President | Russians boycott Olympic Games<br>Famine in Ethiopia<br>Doctors identify AIDS virus<br>Chemical factory disaster in India |
| PLO hijack Italian cruise ship<br>Football riot kills 41 fans in Belgium | Orson Welles, actor and film maker, dies | Live Aid concerts for Ethiopia<br>Earthquake in Mexico kills thousands<br>Wreck of *Titanic* found on sea bed |
| US planes bomb Libya<br>Arab terrorists plant bombs in Paris | Olaf Palme, Swedish Prime Minister, assassinated<br>Clint Eastwood, actor, enters politics | Chernobyl nuclear reactor disaster<br>US space shuttle explodes on take-off<br>'Big Bang' in the City of London |
| Indian and Sri Lankan troops fight Tamils<br>Afghan rebels fight on against Russians | Andy Warhol, artist, dies<br>German teenager flies alone to Moscow | Stock markets of the world crash<br>£24 million paid for a Van Gogh<br>Fierce storms devastate Britain |
| Russian troops leave Afghanistan<br>Iran and Iraq end their war | Russian space station *Mir* launched<br>President Reagan broadcasts to Russia<br>George Bush elected US President<br>Benazir Bhutto elected in Pakistan | US ship shoots down Iranian airliner<br>US airliner explodes over Scotland<br>Australian bicentennial celebrations<br>Piper Alpha gas rig explodes |
| Students protest in China<br>Democracy demonstrations in East Germany and Georgia, USSR<br>Revolution in Romania | ANC's Walter Sisulu freed from jail<br>President Ceausescu of Romania executed<br>Vaclav Havel, playwright, elected Czech President | San Francisco hit by earthquake<br>Shakespeare's Globe theatre found |

# 1980

# HOSTAGE RESCUE BIDS

## US TROOPS FAIL TO RESCUE HOSTAGES

**April 25, Tehran, Iran** A secret force of American commandos has failed in its attempt to rescue a group of US hostages. Nearly 100 hostages are being held in the occupied US embassy here in Iran. They were taken hostage in the embassy in November last year. The rescue mission by the US Delta Force ended in disaster when two aircraft collided and burst into flames. They were refuelling in the Iranian desert.

Helicopters carrying American troops had taken off from an aircraft carrier sailing in the Persian Gulf. They were still some 300 km (186 miles) from their target when disaster struck. Eight US servicemen died in the accident. The mission was immediately called off.

## FAILURE A BLOW TO CARTER

**April 26, Washington DC** President Carter has taken the blame for the failure of the rescue mission. This may affect his chances of being re-elected later this year. Abroad, the desert disaster has spoiled America's all-powerful image. In Iran, the Ayatollah Khomeini will be pleased that America, which he calls 'the Great Satan', has lost face.

# SAS RESCUE LONDON EMBASSY HOSTAGES

**May 5, London** A team from the Special Air Service (SAS) today had a dramatic shoot-out with armed terrorists. Six days ago, the Iranian embassy in London was seized by anti-Khomeini terrorists. They demanded that political prisoners in Iran be released. The people inside the embassy, diplomats and visitors alike, were taken hostage.

This afternoon, black-clad figures slid down the roof and crashed through the windows. For a few minutes the crackle of automatic gunfire could be heard, and then it was all over. The hostages were free, and all but one of the terrorists were dead.

Police officers keep the public at a safe distance as SAS men re-take the Iranian embassy. The assault ends a six-day siege of the embassy, held by Iranian terrorists.

# WAR BETWEEN IRAN AND IRAQ

**Sept 25, Abadan, Iran** Iraqi tanks yesterday led an attack on Iran. The Iraqi army crossed the border in several places and began advancing into Iranian territory. One of the first places to be attacked was the world's largest oil refinery at Abadan.

Relations between the two Arab countries have been bad for some time. One of the main causes of dispute is the Sha'at al Arab waterway, which forms part of the border between them. The Iraqi leader, Saddam Hussein, says only the Iraqis can use this vital outlet to the sea.

# FREE TRADE UNION IN POLAND

**Sept 22, Gdansk, Poland** Polish workers have won the right to form an independent trade union. The government gave in to workers' demands after months of strikes. The new trade union is called Solidarity. Its leader is Lech Walesa, an electrician at the Gdansk shipyards. (Gdansk was once known as Danzig.) Solidarity is the first independent trade union ever to be permitted in a Communist country.

Ronald Reagan and his wife Nancy

# MARXIST PRIME MINISTER FOR ZIMBABWE

**March 4, Harare, Zimbabwe** Robert Mugabe has been elected Prime Minister of newly independent Zimbabwe. He is the first black leader of this African country (which was formerly called Rhodesia, and ruled by the white minority). Mr. Mugabe is a Marxist and a believer in black majority rule. However, he is expected to make concessions to the rich whites who control most of Zimbabwe's industry and agriculture.

The statue of Cecil Rhodes, founder of Rhodesia, is pulled down by jubilant Zimbabweans.

# CARTER LOSES US ELECTION

**Nov 4, Washington DC, USA** The Republican candidate, Ronald Reagan, has been elected the next US President. The new Vice-President is to be George Bush. Reagan defeated Jimmy Carter by a large majority. Carter lost popularity after the failure of the hostage rescue attempt in April.

Both newcomers have been in politics for some time. Reagan has served as governor of California, and Bush was formerly head of the CIA. Before entering politics Reagan was a film actor.

# NEWS IN BRIEF . . .

## SMALLPOX A DISEASE OF THE PAST

**May 8, Geneva, Switzerland** The World Health Organization today announced that smallpox has been wiped out. Their worldwide vaccination campaign has been a success. For centuries this infectious disease has killed most of its victims, and left survivors with pockmarked faces. The last reported case was in Somalia in the late 1970s. Scientists now believe that the threat of smallpox has gone for ever.

Daley Thompson of the United Kingdom at the Moscow Olympics

## VOLCANO ERUPTS IN AMERICA

**May 19, Washington, USA** A dormant volcano has erupted, killing at least eight people. After rumbling for weeks, Mount St. Helens finally exploded today, showering ash over a wide area. In places the ash fall is more than 10 m (31 ft.) deep. Houses and cars have been completely buried. Floods and mudslides caused by the eruption have also caused much damage.

## MAN OF 1000 FACES DIES

**July 24, Switzerland** The British actor Peter Sellers has died after a short illness. Sellers was one of the world's best-loved comedy actors, and was a complete master of disguise. In some of his films he played several different roles. His was the voice behind several weird characters in the radio show The Goons. His most famous character was the accident-prone French detective Inspector Clouseau, in the Pink Panther films.

## US BOYCOTTS MOSCOW OLYMPICS

**Aug 3, Moscow** The 22nd Olympic Games ended today. There have been no competitors from the United States, West Germany or Kenya. These countries stayed away in protest at the Russian invasion of Afghanistan. Some individual athletes from other countries also refused to attend. Daley Thompson, Steve Ovett and Sebastian Coe of Britain all won gold medals.

## PERSONAL STEREO SUCCESS

**Dec 31, Tokyo, Japan** The most popular accessory in the world this year is the 'Walkman' personal stereo system produced by the Sony company. 'Walkman' is a tiny cassette player, equipped with a pair of lightweight headphones. Easily carried on a belt, 'Walkman' enables active people to enjoy music while they walk, jog, cycle or travel on public transport.

## JOHN LENNON SHOT

**Dec 8, New York** Ex-Beatle John Lennon has been shot dead in a New York street. Lennon, aged 40, was returning home with his wife Yoko Ono, when a gunman opened fire at close range. Police have arrested the killer, who claims to be one of John Lennon's greatest fans.

# 1981

Jan 21    US hostages released from Tehran
March 30  President Reagan wounded
May 13    Pope shot by gunman
Oct 6     President Sadat assassinated

# LEADERS ARE GUNMEN'S TARGETS

## POPE WOUNDED IN ASSASSINATION ATTEMPT

**May 13, Vatican City, Italy**  Pope John Paul II has been seriously wounded by a lone gunman. The Pope was riding in an open-topped vehicle when shots rang out. He was rushed to hospital, where surgeons removed four bullets. Doctors say that the Pope is expected to make a full recovery.

Immediately after the shooting, police arrested Mehmet Agca, a 23-year old Armenian. Agca is wanted by the Turkish police for the murder of a leading Turkish journalist. He claims he shot the Pope as a protest against the warlike behaviour of the two superpowers. Many people think there was another motive, however. They suspect that Agca may have been hired by an East European country. Communist governments are known to be angry at the Pope's support for the Polish Solidarity trade union movement.

# PRESIDENT REAGAN SHOT

**March 30, Washington DC, USA**  A man today shot and wounded President Reagan and three other people. The shots were fired as the President left a hotel in town. Secret Service agents immediately overpowered the attacker and handed him over to police. The President was taken to hospital where a bullet was removed from near his heart. Hospital spokesmen say that the President is now out of danger. He is in good spirits, and is said to be making jokes with his doctors.

# SADAT OF EGYPT ASSASSINATED

**Oct 6, Cairo, Egypt**  President Anwar Sadat has been shot dead during a military parade. The assassins were dressed in army uniforms, and so far no one knows who they were.

President Sadat won the Nobel Peace Prize for making peace with Israel. But in doing so, he made many enemies in the Arab world. Many people wanted him dead. Most likely, he was killed by members of the Muslim Brotherhood, an Islamic fundamentalist organization. The Egyptian Vice-President, Hosni Murbarak, takes over as head of state until elections can be held.

A security man shouts instructions after the assassination of President Sadat.

11

# TEHRAN HOSTAGES RELEASED

**Jan 21, Tehran, Iran** The American embassy hostages have been released. Last night, they were flown to Algeria, from where they will be returned to the United States. The hostages spent a total of 444 days in captivity. They were released on the day after President Reagan's inauguration. Ayatollah Khomeini meant this as a final snub to ex-President Carter, who failed to rescue the hostages. There have been noisy celebrations in America.

# NEW PRIME MINISTER FOR POLAND

**Feb 9, Warsaw, Poland** There are still strikes and unrest in Poland, even though workers have the Solidarity trade union to back them. The Communist leaders have appointed General Jaruzelski as Prime Minister. Jaruzelski is a moderate, and may have been chosen because Solidarity might agree to negotiate with him. However, he is also a soldier. Maybe the authorities are planning military conflict with the new trade union.

# ATTEMPTED COUP IN SPAIN

**Feb 24, Madrid, Spain** Rebel members of the Civil Guard yesterday took over the Spanish parliament building. They fired automatic weapons, and took about 350 MPs hostage. At first, some army units seemed to be supporting the rebels. However, they returned to their barracks after a television broadcast by King Juan Carlos. Shortly afterwards, the Civil Guards surrendered to the authorities. They are believed to be right-wing extremists who want an end to parliamentary government in Spain.

# NEW POLITICAL PARTY IN BRITAIN

**March 26, London** A group of British MPs have launched a new political party: the Social Democratic Party (SDP). They all used to belong to the Labour Party. The group includes four former cabinet ministers. The leading members of the group are Shirley Williams, Roy Jenkins, Bill Rogers and David Owen. The British press have nicknamed them the 'Gang of Four'. The party has attracted many former Labour Party members worried by Labour's socialist policies.

# GISCARD OUT – MITTERRAND IN

**May 10, Paris, France** The socialist politician François Mitterrand has been elected President of France. He defeated Giscard d'Estaing by a decisive majority. Mitterrand is the first socialist to lead France for more than 20 years. Although he will follow left-wing policies at home, he is a firm supporter of the NATO alliance.

# MORE RIOTS IN BRITAIN

**July 11, London** Riots flared in several cities last night. It has been called 'Britain's night of anarchy'. In London, Liverpool, Birmingham and other cities, police and rioters fought pitched battles. Rioters burned cars and looted shops. Many people were injured.

This is the third major outbreak of rioting this year. In April, the streets of Brixton in London were set ablaze in protest at police harassment. Dozens of houses burned down, and hundreds were injured. In May, there were serious riots in Ulster after the death in prison of IRA hunger-striker Bobby Sands.

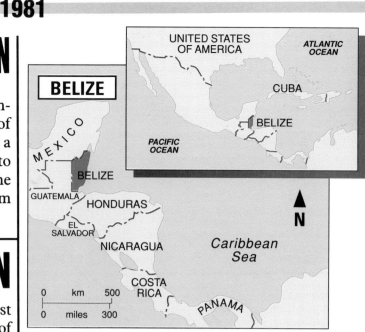

# INDEPENDENCE FOR BELIZE

**Sept 20, Belize City, Belize** Belize in Central America has become independent. It was formerly British Honduras. Months of difficult negotiations were held with Honduras and Guatemala. These neighbouring countries have threatened to invade. As a result, British troops will be staying on in order to protect Belize's borders.

# MARTIAL LAW IN POLAND

**Dec 14, Warsaw, Poland** In a surprise move, General Jaruzelski yesterday imposed martial law to crush the Solidarity movement. Tanks have been used to break up demonstrations and deter protesting crowds. Several workers have been killed. Thousands of Solidarity members, including leader Lech Walesa, have been arrested. The Catholic Church in Poland continues to support Solidarity.

# FIRST SPACE SHUTTLE LAUNCH

**April 11, Florida, USA** The first US space shuttle *Columbia* was today launched like a rocket into orbit. The shuttle belongs to a new generation of re-usable spacecraft. After its three-day space mission, *Columbia* will re-enter Earth's atmosphere, and land like an aeroplane. The astronauts appeared live on television from the spacecraft.

# NEWS IN BRIEF . . .

## PRINCE CHARLES MARRIES

**July 29, London** The Queen's eldest son, Charles, Prince of Wales, today married Lady Diana Spencer. The ceremony at St. Paul's Cathedral was televised to an estimated world-wide audience of 700 million. The royal romance and engagement have been front-page news for many months in the popular press. This latest royal wedding has started rumours that the Queen will soon abdicate. If she did so, her eldest son would become King Charles III.

## BOB MARLEY DIES

**May 11, Florida, USA** The Jamaican reggae musician, Bob Marley, has died in hospital of cancer. Marley, aged 36, was the king of reggae, with its slow, insistent beat. He was popular with both black and white audiences and had a world-wide following. Recently, Marley had become involved in Jamaican politics. He worked for peace and unity between rival political parties.

## BRITISH PETROL NOW IN LITRES

**Sept 1, London** British motorists will no longer fill up their cars with petrol measured in gallons. From today, petrol pumps will serve it priced in litres. This is the latest move in Britain's slow progress towards use of the metric system. Many people want to continue with the old imperial measurements. But membership of the Common Market means that Britain must go metric like the rest of Europe. Soon milk will also be sold in litres.

## NEW IMMUNE DEFICIENCY DISEASE

**Dec 30, Los Angles, USA** Doctors here and in New York have identified a new killer disease. Victims lose weight rapidly and then die from infection. The disease affects the human immune system. Over 150 cases have been reported this year, nearly all of them among male homosexuals.

## CHRISTY BROWN DIES

**Sept 7, Dublin** The Irish writer and artist, Christy Brown, has died at the age of 48. Brown was a remarkable character. He was almost completely paralysed from birth, and could only move his left foot. Typing just with the toes of one foot, he wrote a best-selling autobiography, *Down All Our Days*.

## 'NO CRUISE' DEMONSTRATION

**Oct 24, London** Over 150,000 peace protestors crowded into London's Hyde Park today. They oppose the deployment of American cruise missiles in Britain. Cruise missiles are the newest American nuclear weapons. With a range of about 1000 km (621 miles) they fly at low level like tiny aircraft and are very hard to detect. The protesters say that having cruise missiles in Britain makes the country a likelier target for attack.

# 1982

| April 2 | Argentina invades Falkland Islands |
| June 14 | Argentine troops surrender |
| Aug 31 | Israel drives PLO out of Beirut |
| Oct 8 | Solidarity banned |
| Nov 10 | Andropov replaces Brezhnev |

# WAR OVER FALKLAND ISLANDS
## FALKLAND ISLANDS INVADED

**April 2, Port Stanley, Falkland Islands** Argentinian troops today invaded these remote British islands in the South Atlantic. About 100 British soldiers were taken prisoner in a daring night attack. The invasion has taken the British government completely by surprise. For many years, Argentina has said it owns the Falkland Islands, which it calls Las Malvinas. However, there were no signs that Argentina was about to invade.

British Prime Minister Margaret Thatcher announced that the government will send a task force of men and ships to retake the Falkland

Islands. When the task force is ready, it will sail 12,500 km (7765 miles) to the South Atlantic.

In Buenos Aires, the Argentinian capital, there are celebrations. Thousands turned out to cheer General Galtieri, the country's military leader, when he announced that Las Malvinas had been recaptured.

HMS *Fearless* leaves for the Falkland Islands as part of the British task force.

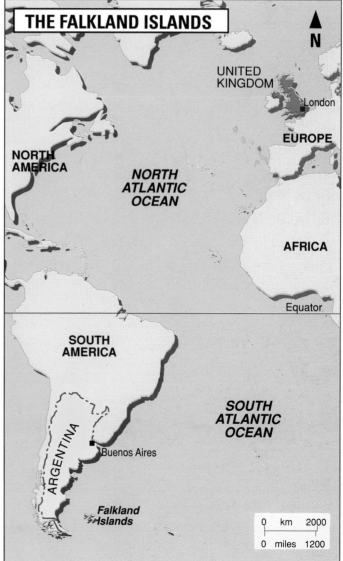

THE FALKLAND ISLANDS

N

UNITED KINGDOM

London

EUROPE

NORTH AMERICA

NORTH ATLANTIC OCEAN

AFRICA

Equator

SOUTH AMERICA

ARGENTINA

Buenos Aires

SOUTH ATLANTIC OCEAN

Falkland Islands

| 0 | km | 2000 |
| 0 | miles | 1200 |

# BRITISH AND ARGENTINIAN WARSHIPS SUNK

**May 4, London** A British destroyer, HMS *Sheffield*, was today destroyed. Twenty men died, and many more were wounded. It was hit by an Exocet missile fired from an Argentinian aircraft. The missile attack seems to be in revenge for the sinking of the Argentinian warship *General Belgrano* two days ago. The *General Belgrano* was the only Argentian warship at sea. It posed a threat to the British task force now on its way to the Falkland Islands. It was sunk by a British submarine, and over 400 Argentinians must have drowned.

# MISSILE ATTACK ON HMS *SHEFFIELD*

**May 6, South Atlantic** "It had a devastating effect. It hit the centre of the ship, the centre of all operations – mechanical, detection, weaponry. It came in at six feet above the water level, damaged two large compartments and exploded outwards and upwards. We only had time to say 'take cover'. The missile hit . . . at hundreds of miles an hour."
(Captain Salt, Commander of HMS *Sheffield*, reported in *The Times*)

# BRITISH TROOPS GO ASHORE

**May 23, Falkland Islands** After two days of heavy fighting, British troops have made a base on the Falkland Islands. The first troops went ashore in San Carlos Bay, and have now moved inland.

The landing site is continually bombed by Argentinian aircraft. Two more British ships were sunk and more have been damaged. British Harrier jet fighters have shot down several Argentinian aircraft. Others have been brought down by SAMs (surface to air missiles) such as Rapier.

# ARGENTINIAN FORCES SURRENDER

**June 14, Port Stanley** The last Argentinian forces in the Falklands surrendered today. They were completely surrounded in the capital, Port Stanley. This final British success follows that of two weeks ago, when paratroops recaptured the Goose Green airfield. In both cases, large numbers of Argentinian soldiers surrendered to smaller and better-equipped British forces. Two-and-a-half months after the Argentinian invasion, the Falkland Islands are once again under British rule.

# UK UNEMPLOYMENT TOPS 3 MILLION

**Jan 28, London** The number of unemployed people in Britain has reached more than 3,000,000 for the first time since the 1930s. In order to fight inflation, the government has tried to control the supply of money. This has in turn forced companies to cut jobs, which has resulted in greater unemployment.

# WOMEN'S PEACE CAMP

**Sept 30, Greenham Common, Britain** A large group of women have established a Peace Camp around the US Air Force base at Greenham Common in Berkshire. The women are protesting about the cruise missiles which are to be stored at the base. Although most of the women are British, there are anti-nuclear supporters from all over Europe.

# ISRAEL EVICTS THE PLO

**Aug 31, Beirut, Lebanon** The Israeli army has forced the Palestine Liberation Organization (PLO) out of Lebanon. For years, the PLO has used Lebanon as a base for attacks on Israel. Today, PLO leader Yasser Arafat left Beirut to join his 7000 fighters in exile. Most of them have gone to sympathetic Arab countries such as Syria, Iraq and Algeria.

Israel invaded Lebanon at the beginning of June. Very soon, the PLO was under siege in its Beirut headquarters. There was also fierce fighting around the PLO strongholds in Sidon and Tyre. Syrian forces were in fierce tank clashes with the Israelis on the road to Damascus. More than 60 Syrian aircraft were shot down. Most of the Lebanese Muslim population, which includes many Palestinian refugees, support the PLO. Christian inhabitants, and members of a Syrian sect called Druse, are against them.

# MASSACRES IN LEBANON

**Sept 17, Beirut**   There has been bloodshed following the PLO's departure from Beirut. Today, Christian militia began murdering the Palestinian refugees in camps at Sabra and Chatila. Already, hundreds of men, women and children are reported dead. Lebanon's Christian Prime Minister was killed earlier this week, and the massacre was a revenge attack. Israeli troops have done nothing to prevent the killings. Some Palestinians say the Israelis helped the Christian militia.

A damaged street in Beirut

# NEW CHANCELLOR FOR W GERMANY

**Oct 1, Bonn, W. Germany**   Helmut Schmidt, the leader of the left-wing Social Democrat party, has been sacked as Chancellor of West Germany. The Bonn parliament today voted to replace him with Helmut Kohl, the leader of the right-wing Christian Democrat party. MPs hope that Christian Democrat policies will reduce public spending and cut unemployment.

# SOLIDARITY BANNED

**Oct 8, Warsaw, Poland**   Solidarity, the independent trade union, has been banned by Poland's Communist government. Spokesmen for the union, which is now illegal, said that they would continue to operate in secret. They urged supporters not to become involved in mass demonstrations that would provoke violence.

# SOCIALIST VICTORY IN SPAIN

**Oct 28, Madrid, Spain**   The Socialist party has won a landslide victory in the Spanish elections. The moderate centre parties appear to have collapsed completely. The new parliament will be sharply divided between a left-wing majority, and a right-wing minority. The new Prime Minister will be Felipe Gonzalez. Aged just 40, he will become Europe's youngest national leader.

# ANDROPOV REPLACES BREZHNEV

**Nov 10, Moscow**   President Leonid Brezhnev has died of a heart attack, aged 75. The new Russian leader will be Yuri Andropov, who was formerly head of the KGB, the Russian secret police. Although Andropov has been tough with his rivals, he is expected to be more liberal in some policies. Brezhnev held very old-fashioned views, and he failed to reform the Russian economy so that it could compete with the West.

Mr. Andropov, the new Russian leader

# NEWS IN BRIEF . . .

## ENGLISH CRICKETERS BANNED

**March 20, London** Fourteen of England's top cricketers have been banned from the national team because they are playing in South Africa. Cricket's ruling body, like those of other sports, has forbidden all sporting contacts with South Africa as a protest against apartheid. The players will not be considered for the England team until 1985.

## CORPORAL PUNISHMENT BANNED

**Feb 25, Strasbourg, France** The European Court has banned the corporal punishment of children without their parents' consent. In effect, this means that schools will no longer be able to punish children by physical methods such as the cane. Most parents support the court's decision, but some still believe that physical punishment is necessary in order to enforce discipline in schools.

## MOONIE LEADER CONVICTED

**May 18, USA** Sun Myung Moon, the leader of the Unification Church, has been found guilty of income tax evasion. Members of the church are often known as 'Moonies'. For many months, Moon has been under investigation because of his extravagant life-style. He receives large donations from religious converts, most of them young people. In a few cases, Moonie groups have been accused of holding people against their will, and brainwashing them into staying and then claiming them as converts.

## ZIMBABWE'S LEADERS SPLIT

**Feb 17, Harare** Since Zimbabwe became independent in 1980, the country's new Prime Minister Robert Mugabe has shared power with the veteran nationalist, Joshua Nkomo. Today Mr. Mugabe dismissed Mr. Nkomo from his cabinet, along with two other ministers. The power struggle in Zimbabwe has ended.

## SILICON CHIP REVOLUTION

**Sept 30, London and New York** Another industrial revolution is in full swing in the industrialized nations. Micro-processors on silicon chips are now being used in workplaces doing enormously varied work. Robots assembling cars, word-processors in offices, information storage on discs, all rely on the 'microchip'.

## E.T. – A LOVABLE ALIEN IS EVERYONE'S FAVOURITE

**Dec 3, Hollywood, USA** The hit film of the year is *E.T. – The Extra-Terrestial*, by Stephen Spielberg. The film is about a being from another world which becomes stranded on earth. The alien is befriended by some children who help it to organize a rescue mission. The film has the irresistible combination of a cute story, a cast of talented child actors, and some dazzling special effects. Children and adults alike are flocking to see *E.T.* The film goes on release in Britain today.

## HISTORIC WRECK OF HENRY VIII'S WARSHIP RAISED

**Oct 11, London** A 450-year old wooden warship has been lifted from the sea bed. The *Mary Rose* sank in Portsmouth harbour in the reign of Henry VIII. Over the years, the wreck became covered in mud, which has preserved the timbers. Now after months of patient work by underwater archaeologists, the hull of the *Mary Rose* has been brought to the surface supported by a strong cradle. Among the objects found on board are cannon, swords, and wooden longbows that still work.

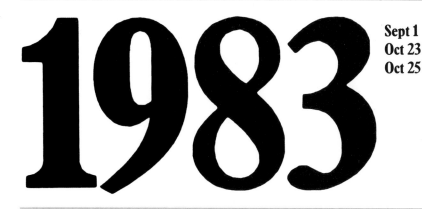

# 1983

Sept 1    South Korean airliner shot down
Oct 23    Lebanese kill US and French troops
Oct 25    US troops invade Grenada

## USA TO HAVE SPACE DEFENCE SYSTEM

**March 23, Washington DC, USA** President Reagan has announced that America is to develop a real-life 'Star Wars' defence system. A system of satellites equipped with lasers and other advanced weapons would shoot down enemy missiles whilst they were still in flight. Reagan claimed that the 'Star Wars' system would end the threat of a surprise nuclear attack. In the future, orbiting satellites would give America a safe protective shield.

A technician at work in a 'Star Wars' research laboratory.

## MRS THATCHER RE-ELECTED

**June 10, London** The Conservative Party has won the British general election, and Mrs. Margaret Thatcher has been re-elected Prime Minister. Despite the growth in unemployment, the Conservatives won the election by a record majority.

One of the main reasons for this success is Mrs. Thatcher herself. She is seen as a strong leader who will stand up for Britain.

## POLITICAL ASSASSINATION AT AIRPORT

**Aug 21, Manila, Philippines** A Filipino opposition leader has been assassinated minutes after he returned from exile. Benigno Aquino had just stepped off a plane from the United States when he was shot dead by a lone gunman. Mr. Aquino was a serious rival to President Marcos, and was going to stand against him soon in an election.

## RUSSIA SHOOTS DOWN KOREAN AIRLINER

**Sept 7, Moscow** Russian jet fighters have shot down a South Korean airliner, killing all 269 passengers and crew. The incident happened a week ago, but the Russian authorities have only just admitted what happened. They claim that the airliner was on a spying mission for the Americans, and was shot down over a secret military base. The Americans deny this, and say that the aircraft had accidentally strayed off course. South Korea has strong links with the USA, but it is unlikely that they would use a civilian aircraft for spying. Did the Russians open fire too hastily?

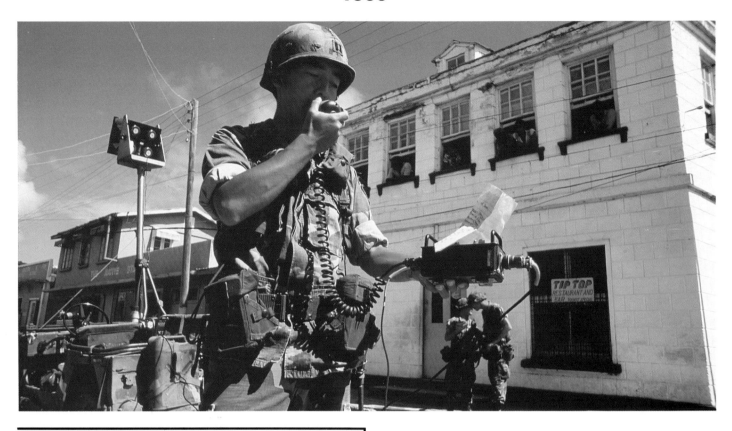

# BEIRUT BOMBERS KILL HUNDREDS

**Oct 23, Beirut, Lebanon** Islamic fundamentalists have killed more than 300 French and American soldiers in two bomb attacks. In both incidents, trucks full of explosives were driven into the military headquarters of peace-keeping forces. The drivers then set off the explosives, killing themselves along with their victims.

The more serious attack was at the US Marine base, where over 250 Americans died. The other attack destroyed a multi-storey building and killed nearly 60 French paratroops. The marines and paratroops were part of the international peace-keeping force that moved into Beirut last year following the Israeli invasion. British and Italian troops are also stationed there, to support the Lebanese army.

Those responsible for the suicide attacks are believed to be Shiite Muslims who claim the Ayatollah Khomeini as their leader. They are opposed to the peace-keeping force because they believe that it supports the Christian militias. Beirut has become one of the most dangerous cities on earth. These attacks are not the only terrorist outrages this year. Earlier, a car bomb destroyed the US embassy.

# US INVADES GRENADA

**Oct 25, St. Georges, Grenada** American combat troops have been sent to the Caribbean island of Grenada. In places, the local people fought the troops, and there have been some casualties.

The American soldiers were sent to restore democratic government to the island. Last week, Grenada's Prime Minister was murdered during what appears to be a Marxist coup. In explaining his reasons for the invasion, US President Reagan pointed to the large numbers of Cuban workers on the island. Mr. Reagan claimed that these workers were in fact Cuban soldiers.

# PLO QUIT LEBANON AGAIN

**Dec 20, Tripoli, Lebanon** Yasser Arafat and the PLO have been forced to leave Lebanon for the second time in two years. This time, they were forced out by the Syrian army.

For the past three weeks, the Syrians and the PLO have fought for control of the Palestinian refugee camps. The better-equipped Syrians won. The PLO are now evacuating to Tunisia under the protection of the United Nations.

# NEWS IN BRIEF . . .

## MOST POPULAR TV SHOW

**Feb 28, USA** A record television audience of 125 million Americans watched the last ever episode of *M.A.S.H.* tonight. *M.A.S.H.* is a long-running situation comedy set in a mobile army hospital during the Korean War. The scripts are extremely clever, and combine witty dialogue with anti-war satire.

## MADONNA'S CLOTHES SET TREND

**Aug 31, USA** Madonna, a young female singer, may have started a new fashion trend that carries on where punk left off. On stage, Madonna has taken to wearing her underwear over the top of her other clothes. Audiences love the idea, and hundreds of teenage girls are now copying the Madonna look. She also uses energetic dance routines on stage. With a voice that is even better than her sense of style, Madonna looks set for great success.

## OIL PRICE CUT

**March 14, London** How the times have changed. In contrast to the oil shortages and energy crisis of the 1970s, there is now a glut of oil and the price is coming down. For the first time in its history, the Organization of Oil Producing Countries (OPEC) has said the price of oil will come down. Some economists believe that the cheapness of oil will cause a boom in the industrialized countries of the world.

## AMERICA'S CUP GOES TO AUSTRALIA

**Sept 23, Rhode Island, USA** For the first time in 132 years, America has lost the America's Cup, the world's most famous yacht racing trophy. Australia is the new holder of the cup, having beaten the USA by just one race. International yacht racing is extremely expensive. The victorious yacht *Australia II* is owned by a millionaire businessman.

The winning Australian crew

## PEACE PRIZE FOR SOLIDARITY LEADER

**Dec 10, Oslo, Norway** Lech Walesa, leader of Poland's Solidarity trade union, has been awarded the Nobel Peace Prize. The Communist authorities have tried to put down the union, sometimes brutally. But Walesa has always kept up his policy of non-violent opposition. By doing so, he has gained the support of the Catholic Church which is against all forms of violence.

## HITLER DIARIES A FAKE!

**May 6, Bonn, West Germany** Two weeks ago, a German magazine published an amazing journalistic scoop: extracts from Adolf Hitler's personal diaries. Hitler was Germany's leader during World War II, and the diaries revealed some fascinating details. Many historians believed the diaries were genuine. Today, however, a panel of experts declared that the diaries were in fact extremely clever forgeries. Police are now looking for the forger who played an elaborate hoax on the press.

# 1984

## STRIKE VIOLENCE IN BRITAIN WORSENS

**May 30, Yorkshire, Britain**   The 12-week strike by the British miners' union is becoming more and more violent. Arthur Scargill, the leader of the National Union of Miners, has not condemned the violence. Yesterday, 70 people were injured when police clashed with striking miners. The miners were on a picket line, trying to prevent coal trucks reaching a steel works. The police wore full riot gear. They finally broke up the group of miners with a charge by policemen on horseback.

The miners' strike shows how sharp are the divisions in British politics. On one level, the miners are striking for better pay and conditions, and to retain jobs. The National Coal Board has said it wants to close up to 20 'uneconomic' pits. There could be 20,000 jobs lost. At a deeper level, the strike is an attack on the government. Mrs. Thatcher's Conservative Party wants to limit the power of British trade unions.

## RUSSIANS BOYCOTT US OLYMPICS

**July 28, Los Angeles, USA**   The Russians and most of their allies are boycotting the Los Angeles Olympic Games. Romania is the only country from the Soviet bloc taking part.

Four years ago, American athletes stayed away from the Moscow Olympics in protest over the Russian invasion of Afghanistan. This year, the Russians are claiming that they are worried about security at the games.

Sports fans all over the world wonder whether the Olympics will ever again be free of the shadow of international politics.

## MRS THATCHER SURVIVES IRA BOMB

**Oct 12, Brighton, England**   Prime Minister Thatcher had a narrow escape early this morning when an IRA bomb exploded at her hotel. Mrs. Thatcher was staying at the Grand Hotel in Brighton for the annual Conservative Party conference. Several senior ministers were also staying at the same hotel.

Four people were killed in the blast, which destroyed four floors of the hotel. Many other guests and staff were injured, some seriously. The police immediately sealed off the area while ambulances took the injured to hospital.

This is the most devastating IRA attack for many years. It casts doubt on the efficiency of police security arrangements. Mrs. Thatcher had a very lucky escape. With a single bomb, the IRA could have wiped out half the British government.

## POLISH PRIEST MURDERED

**Oct 30, Warsaw, Poland**   A Catholic priest, who was an active supporter of Solidarity, has been murdered. The body of Father Jerzy Popieluszko was found in a reservoir earlier today. Father Popieluszko was a close friend of Lech Walesa, the Solidarity leader. He had spoken openly in his church against the government.

It is widely believed that the Polish secret police were behind the killing. If it is true, this was a bad mistake on the part of the authorities. The death of Father Popieluszko will unite Solidarity with the Polish Catholic Church in opposition to the Communist government and its policies. Solidarity continues to avoid violent demonstrations.

The Golden Temple at Amritsar in India, where Sikh extremists fought with Indian troops

# MRS GANDHI ASSASSINATED

**Oct 31, New Delhi, India** Indira Gandhi, Prime Minister of India, was assassinated by her own bodyguards today. She was on her way to a TV interview when two Sikh bodyguards shot her at close range. The new Indian Prime Minister is to be her second son, Rajiv Gandhi.

The assassination was a revenge attack. Mrs. Gandhi had allowed the Indian army to evict militant Sikhs from the Golden Temple at Amritsar in June this year. Over 700 Sikhs died during four days of heavy fighting against tanks and artillery. Sikhs follow a different religion from the rest of India, which is mostly Hindu. Sikhs are traditionally a warrior people. Recently, Sikh extremists have been demanding their own independent Sikh state. Mrs. Gandhi and her government were firmly against these separatist ideas. Already there have been revenge attacks on Sikhs by Hindu mobs, killing, burning and looting.

# FAMINE IN EAST AFRICA

**October, Addis Ababa, Ethiopia** Seven million people here face starvation in one of the worst famines of modern times. Drought has again caused the crops to fail. The situation is made worse by a civil war in the north of the country.

When news of the famine reached the outside world, offers of help poured in from governments and from the general public. However, the authorities here are inefficient and suspicious. So far, few of the relief shipments have reached the people of Ethiopia.

# NEWS IN BRIEF . . .

## BRITISH SKATERS ARE OLYMPIC STARS
**February 14, Sarajevo, Yugoslavia** British skaters Jayne Torvill and Christopher Dean have won the gold medal for ice dancing at the Winter Olympics.

## MYSTERY DISEASE EXPLAINED
**April 23, Washington DC, USA** Doctors have isolated the virus that causes the killer disease AIDS (Acquired Immune Deficiency Syndrome).

AIDS was first reported in 1981 among male homosexuals. However, doctors now say that AIDS is spreading to other sections of society. Although they have found the virus, they admit that it may be many years before they can find a cure.

## LEWIS GOES FOR GOLD
**August 31, Los Angeles, USA** Star of the main Olympic Games was American athlete Carl Lewis. He won three gold medals for sprinting, and set an Olympic record for the 200 m. Lewis also won a gold medal in the long jump, giving him a total of four.

## RONALD REAGAN RE-ELECTED
**Nov 6, Washington DC, USA** President Reagan has been re-elected to another four-year term of office. He beat the Democratic contender, Walter Mondale, by a huge majority. Six out of every ten Americans voted for Mr. Reagan.

Reagan is one of the most popular Presidents this century. The former film star is known as the 'Great Communicator'. Many Americans particularly admire his tough, straightforward speeches on US foreign policy.

## CHEMICAL DISASTER AT BHOPAL
**Dec 10, Bhopal, India** A leak at a chemical factory has killed at least 2500 people, and injured as many as 250,000. A cloud of poisonous gas escaped from the factory. It spread over the surrounding area, where thousands of people live. Many of the injured have been blinded.

Local people are angry with the American owners. They say that not enough attention was paid to safety precautions in the factory.

## THRILLING THE WORLD
**Dec 31, Los Angeles, USA** Pop star of the year is 26-year-old American singer Michael Jackson. Formerly a child star with the Jackson Five during the 1970s, Jackson now has a hugely successful solo career. His latest album 'Thriller' has broken all previous records by selling more than 35 million copies around the world.

## BHOPAL VICTIM DESCRIBES DISASTER
**Dec 6, India** "We were choking and our eyes were burning. We could barely see the road through the fog, and sirens were blaring. We didn't know which way to run. Everybody was very confused. Mothers didn't know their children had died, children didn't know their mothers had died, and men didn't know their whole families had died."

(Ahmed Khan, quoted in *The Times*)

# 1985

## GORBACHEV COMES TO POWER

**March 11, Moscow**   Mikhail Gorbachev is the new leader of Russia. He replaces the elderly Konstantin Chernenko who was in power for only 13 months. Chernenko took over when Andropov died last year. At 56, Gorbachev is the youngest member of the Russian leadership, and he is expected to be in favour of economic reform.

The Russian economy is extremely inefficient, and there are always shortages of basic supplies in the shops. Mr. Gorbachev will want factories to produce more consumer goods, and fewer military products. This could make him unpopular with Russian military chiefs.

## FOOTBALL RIOT KILLS 41 FANS

**May 29, Brussels, Belgium**   English football hooligans have been blamed for the deaths of 41 Italian and Belgian spectators at the Heysel stadium. The trouble started before the European Cup Final between teams from England and Italy. A crowd of English supporters charged at a group of Italian fans, causing a stampede. Most of the dead were crushed by a wall that collapsed under the weight of bodies; others were trampled to death. A group of English fans has been detained.

English football fans have a reputation for violence and drunkenness. This latest incident is likely to result in English teams being banned from European competitions.

## 'LIVE AID' FOR ETHIOPIA

**July 7, London and Philadelphia**   Thanks to linked world-wide television, one-third of the world's population watched two pop concerts for charity today. Throughout the day, rock and pop celebrities asked viewers to give money for famine relief in Ethiopia. Altogether about £40 million was raised.

The concerts were the idea of Bob Geldof, who organized the Band Aid record 'Do they know its Christmas?' that was a huge hit last Christmas. Like the concerts, all the proceeds of the record went to Ethiopia. As a result of his charity work, Geldof has become internationally famous.

Bob Geldof asks fans to give money, at the Live Aid concert in London.

# EARTHQUAKE IN MEXICO

**Sept 20, Mexico City** A devastating earthquake hit the world's largest city yesterday. More than 2000 people are reported killed, and thousands more have been injured. Many lie trapped beneath piles of rubble. The earthquake struck near the centre of the city, and dozens of multi-storey buildings have collapsed. Mexican rescue squads are working night and day looking for survivors. Several foreign governments have sent help.

# PLO HIJACK CRUISE SHIP

**Oct 7, Rome, Italy** Gunmen of the Palestine Liberation Organization have seized the *Achille Lauro*, an Italian cruise ship. They are holding 450 passengers hostage. One American passenger has already been killed. The hijackers are demanding the release of Palestinian prisoners from Israeli jails. However, the Israeli government is very unlikely to give in to their demands.

# ITALY LETS HIJACKERS GO FREE

**Oct 17, Rome, Italy** After a bizarre sequence of events, the PLO hijackers have been allowed to go free. The gunmen surrendered in return for an aircraft which would take them to Tunisia. After taking off, they were forced down by American jet fighters and landed in Sicily. The Palestinians were arrested by the Italians, and were then allowed to go free. The US government protested strongly. The Italian government has resigned.

# WRECK OF *TITANIC* FOUND

**Sept 3, Paris** A joint French-American underwater team has found the wreck of the *Titanic*, 4000 metres below the surface of the Atlantic Ocean. The *Titanic* was hailed as 'unsinkable' when it was launched in 1912. But on the very first voyage, it hit an iceberg and sank, with the loss of over 1500 lives. Scientists from the team say that most of the huge ship is lying in one piece on the sea bed. It appears to be in fairly good condition.

# ANGLO-IRISH AGREEMENT SIGNED

**Nov 15, Belfast, Northern Ireland** The British and Irish governments have signed a historic agreement. In future, the government of the Irish Republic will be allowed a say in British policy towards the province of Northern Ireland. There will also be closer co-operation between British and Irish security forces. Protestant politicians in Ulster are strongly against the agreement.

The Rev. Ian Paisley attacks the agreement.

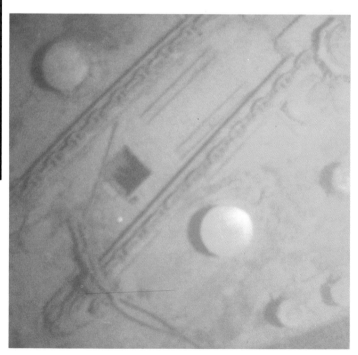

Anchor chains can be seen on the bow of the *Titanic*, thousands of metres down on the sea bed.

# NEWS IN BRIEF . . .

## ELECTRIC THREE-WHEELER MAKES DEBUT

**Jan 10, London** British businessman Sir Clive Sinclair has unveiled his latest invention. It is an electric tricycle called the C5. Sinclair describes the C5 as the answer to city traffic problems and pollution. Powered by batteries, the C5 is cheap and clean to run. However, critics say the C5 is not a practical vehicle, it is more of a toy. An electric city car is a good idea, but the C5 is not likely to prove the right design.

## AIDS EPIDEMIC DECLARED

**Sept 13, Geneva, Switzerland** The World Health Organization has said that there is now a worldwide epidemic of AIDS. Many countries have begun health education programmes to help fight the spread of the disease. In some places, AIDS warnings now appear on television. Although we now understand how the virus is transmitted, there is no known cure for the disease.

## FRENCH AGENTS JAILED

**Nov 21, Auckland, New Zealand** Two French secret agents have been jailed for sinking the ship *Rainbow Warrior* and killing one of the crew. *Rainbow Warrior* belonged to the environmental organization Greenpeace. The ship was sunk here four months ago, by a bomb planted under the hull. *Rainbow Warrior* had often been used to disrupt French nuclear weapons tests in the Pacific Ocean. The New Zealand authorities believe that the ship was sunk on the orders of the French government. One of the agents sent to prison today was a French army diving instructor.

## MIXED MARRIAGE IN SOUTH AFRICA

**June 15, Pretoria** South Africa's first mixed marriage, between people of different races, took place today. Two months ago, the government said that the ban on mixed marriages was over. Despite such changes in the laws which uphold the apartheid regime, a two-tier system is still in force here. Blacks and coloured people are not full citizens because they cannot vote.

## CONTRACEPTIVES LEGALIZED IN IRELAND

**Feb 20, Dublin, Ireland** The Dail, the Irish parliament, has voted to allow contraceptives to be sold in shops. Ireland is strongly influenced by the Catholic Church, which does not condone artificial contraception. Previously, Irish people could only obtain contraceptives from doctors. Now they will be able to buy them in supermarkets and shops, as in other European countries.

## ORSON WELLES DIES

**Oct 10, Hollywood, USA** Orson Welles, the brilliant but erratic American film maker, has died at the age of 70. Welles will be best remembered for *Citizen Kane*, which is considered by many to be the finest film ever made. Welles both directed the film and appeared in the leading role.

## SURPRISE BOOKER WINNER

**Oct 31, London** At London's Guildhall tonight a winner was announced of this year's Booker Prize for Fiction. The New Zealander Keri Hulme won the £15,000 prize for her first novel, *The Bone People*. She beat more well-known writers including Iris Murdoch, Jan Morris and Doris Lessing. Keri Hulme, a Maori, deals with the disturbing ideas of love and violence in personal relationships. The book is described as a long prose poem about Maori myths. Previous winners include Salman Rushdie for *Midnight's Children* in 1981.

# 1986

# NUCLEAR DISASTER IN RUSSIA
## CHERNOBYL REACTOR EXPLODES

**May 1, Chernobyl, Russia**  A reactor at a Russian nuclear power station has exploded and caught fire. Troops and emergency services are making desperate efforts to put out the flames. The task is extremely dangerous because of radioactivity from the damaged reactor. Some of the firefighters are certain to die from radiation poisoning.

The explosion happened five days ago at Chernobyl in southern Russia. It is the most serious nuclear accident ever known. Thousands of local people have been evacuated, because of the dangers of radiation. Experts say that radioactivity from Chernobyl will drift across Western Europe, contaminating food supplies.

A helicopter sprays decontaminates at the Chernobyl nuclear power plant.

# CONTAMINATION SPREADS ACROSS EUROPE

**June 20, London**  The British government has banned the slaughter of sheep for food in parts of northern England. Tests have shown that the animals were contaminated with radiation from Chernobyl. Other European governments are taking similar precautions. In Poland, the authorities have banned the use of milk from certain areas.

Shopkeepers have been quick to react. Some are now using Geiger counters to prove to customers that their goods are uncontaminated by radiation.

# SPACE SHUTTLE EXPLODES

**Jan 28, Cape Kennedy, USA**  The space shuttle *Challenger* exploded 70 seconds after it was launched this morning. The shuttle was engulfed in a ball of flame, and all seven astronauts on board were killed. One of them, Christa McAuliffe, was the first ordinary American citizen to be sent into space. She was a schoolteacher.

The *Challenger* accident is the most serious setback ever suffered by the US space programme. All further shuttle flights have been postponed until scientists have discovered the exact cause of the disaster.

# MARCOS FLEES PHILIPPINES

**Feb 25, Manila, Philippines** President Marcos has been toppled from power by the widow of an assassinated politician. The new leader of the Philippines is Mrs. Corazon (Cory) Aquino.

Earlier this month, Marcos rigged the elections in which Mrs. Aquino was a candidate, and declared himself the winner. This afternoon, crowds of Aquino supporters stormed Marcos' palace. He and his wife escaped by helicopter under cover of darkness, leaving Mrs. Aquino in charge of the country. During his 20 years in power, Marcos is believed to have stolen millions of dollars from the national treasury.

Mrs. Corazon Aquino with her delighted supporters

# SWEDISH PM ASSASSINATED

**Feb 28, Stockholm, Sweden** Olaf Palme, the Swedish Prime Minister, was shot dead tonight. The assassin escaped on foot, and the Swedish police have launched a widespread search for the killer. Mr. Palme was walking home from a cinema when the attack took place.

# US PLANES BOMB LIBYA

**April 15, Tripoli, Libya** American bombers have carried out a series of air attacks against what they call 'terrorist targets' here. Libya's President Gadaffi had a narrow escape when bombs fell near his palace, and his daughter was killed.

The attacks were in retaliation for Libya's involvement in the recent terrorist bombing of US servicemen in Germany.

# 'IRANGATE' SCANDAL IN USA

**Nov 30, Washington DC, USA** A political scandal threatens the career of US President Reagan. The President and his advisors are accused of making secret arms deals with Iran. In return for arms, the Iranians helped release US hostages held in Lebanon. Money from the deals was sent to right-wing Contra rebels in Nicaragua. This new scandal has been dubbed 'Irangate' by the press.

# OPEN FOR INDEPENDENCE DAY

**July 4, New York** The Statue of Liberty was open to visitors today after being refurbished. The famous landmark re-opened on its 100th anniversary, and on Independence Day. America's great symbol of hope was presented to the nation one hundred years ago today. This morning President Reagan surveyed 20 US warships in New York harbour, and lunched with France's President François Mitterrand.

# NEWS IN BRIEF . . .

## HALLEY'S COMET INVESTIGATED

**February 28, Europe** Halley's comet is now visible in the night skies, but it is not as bright as expected. Astronomers have been waiting a long time for a view of the comet, which appears in our skies only every 76 years. It is named after Edmond Halley, who first realized it was a comet. This time around, scientists have a new way of looking. A special space probe, *Giotto*, was launched in July last year to meet the comet. *Giotto* will pass within 5000 km (3100 miles) of Halley's comet, and transmit pictures back to earth.

## ANOTHER ACTOR IN POLITICS

**April 8, California, USA** Another American film actor has gone into politics. Clint Eastwood has been elected Mayor of Carmel, a California tourist resort. Eastwood rose to stardom in 'spaghetti' westerns during the 1960s. Later, he played the gun-happy detective in *Dirty Harry* and its sequels. The job of the mayor is only part-time, however. Eastwood will continue to make movies, both as actor and director.

## HENRY MOORE DIES

**Aug 31, London** British sculptor Henry Moore died today. Moore is famous for his massive, curving stone shapes pierced by holes. During World War II, he made many drawings of people sheltering in the London Underground from air raids, and these influenced his later work. Many of his sculptures are not in art galleries. They are sited in open spaces in cities and in the countryside.

## BIG BANG IN LONDON

**Oct 27, London** Today was 'Big Bang' day in the City of London, the financial district also called the Square Mile. In future there will be fewer official controls over dealings in shares. Today the London Stock Exchange's new computerized share dealing system came into use. After initial troubles, the new system looks like being a success.

## FLYING AROUND THE WORLD

**Dec 12, California, USA** Two Americans, one the daughter of a test pilot, have just completed the first non-stop flight around the world without refuelling. Their oddly-shaped *Voyager* aircraft flew for nine days on a single load of fuel. With its huge wingspan, it operates like a glider. During their long flight, pilots Richard Rutan and Jeana Yeager took it in turns to sleep.

*Voyager* took off on its round-the-world flight with its hollow, carbon fibre wings full of fuel.

# 1987

## REFORMS ANNOUNCED IN RUSSIA

**Jan 29, Moscow**   President Gorbachev has called for greater democracy in Russian politics. He said that central control and lack of choice were to blame for the stagnation of the Russian economy. In future, Gorbachev wants voters to have a choice of candidates in local elections. During his speech, the Russian president used two key words to summarize his proposed reforms: *glasnost* and *perestroika*.

*Glasnost* means openness. If Russia is to develop, the authorities must allow greater freedom of information and criticism. At present, all state information is secret. Open criticism of the government can land citizens in jail. In the past, dissidents have even been confined in mental hospitals.

*Perestroika* means reconstruction. This refers to the task of transforming the Russian economy and political system. Factories need to be re-equipped with modern machinery, and the people must be

Mr. Gorbachev on a recent visit to Prague

given a greater say in deciding government policy.

President Gorbachev will need to be very cautious in making these changes. Many of the older members of the Communist Party are bitterly opposed to any type of reform. They believe that any relaxation of control will bring about a total collapse of the Communist system in Russia.

## IRANIAN PILGRIMS GO ON RAMPAGE

**July 30, Mecca, Saudi Arabia**   Iranian pilgrims visiting Mecca were involved in serious rioting today. The Saudi Arabian police opened fire on the rioters, and more than 100 are believed to have been killed.

The hadj, or pilgrimage to Mecca, is an annual event open to Muslims from all over the world. Muslims try to make the hadj at least once in a lifetime. The riots began when thousands of Iranian fundamentalists used the hadj for demonstrations against America and Israel.

## MUJAHADDIN CONTINUE STRUGGLE

**Sept 30, Kandahar, Afghanistan**   Twenty mujahaddin (freedom fighters) gathered in the shadows around a Russian army post during a recent attack. Some of them carried captured Russian weapons. Others had guns bought with money sent from rich Muslim countries such as Saudi Arabia. At a signal, they fired rockets and machine-guns at the Russians, then vanished into the night.

After nearly seven years of military occupation, the Russians are still no nearer to subduing the mujahaddin, despite their helicopters and tanks.

# HEAVY FIGHTING IN SRI LANKA

**Oct 11, Jafna, Sri Lanka**   Indian troops are engaged in heavy fighting against Tamil Tiger guerrillas. Indian tanks are being used in house-to-house fighting in the Tamil stronghold of Jafna. The Indians came to Sri Lanka to enforce a ceasefire between the Tamils and government forces, and they are now trying to disarm the Tigers.

The Tamil Tigers want a separate Tamil state. For several years they have been using terror tactics against the Sri Lankan government. Open warfare broke out earlier this year. Thousands of people, many of them civilians, have been killed.

# WORLD-WIDE STOCK MARKET CRASH

**Oct 19, London, New York, Tokyo**   Stock markets around the world have tumbled today. It is already being called 'Black Monday'. The trouble began on Friday with the panic selling of shares in New York. After the weekend, the selling continued and spread to other financial centres. In New York, stocks lost more than 20 per cent of their value today. In London, prices fell by 10 per cent.

Experts are blaming the size of the crash on computerized dealing systems. Once the market dropped, the computers were programmed to sell everything. The crash follows five years of rising markets, and many people had become used to the idea that stocks were an easy way to make money. Millions of investors around the world have suddenly become poorer. Some financial companies are certain to go out of business.

# FIJI GOES INDEPENDENT

**Oct 15, Nadi, Fiji**   Fiji is to become an independent republic, Colonel Rambuka announced today. Rambuka has been Fiji's leader since he seized power in May. His coup was supported by most of the native Fijians, who felt threatened by the island's Indian population. Half the people living in Fiji are Indians, but they had nearly all the seats in Fiji's parliament. Colonel Rambuka says he will give power back to the native population.

# NUCLEAR ARMS REDUCTION TREATY

**Dec 8, Washington DC, USA**   President Reagan and President Gorbachev have signed the first treaty that will reduce the number of nuclear missiles. Both superpowers will dismantle their short and medium range missiles. This includes the cruise missiles kept in Britain and other European countries. These moves towards nuclear arms reduction have been welcomed throughout the world. It seems the Cold War is nearly over.

# NEWS IN BRIEF . . .

## ANDY WARHOL DIES

**Feb 22, New York** The most famous exponent of Pop Art died in hospital tonight. During the Sixties and Seventies, Warhol was among the most influential artists in the world. He will be best remembered for his paintings of soup cans, and his images of Marilyn Monroe. But Warhol was more than just a painter and film maker. He was a philosopher of this age of the mass media. He said that in the future, television would make everybody famous for 15 minutes.

## MILLIONS FOR A VAN GOGH

**March 30, London** A painting of a bowl of flowers has been sold to a Japanese insurance company for over £24 million. *Sunflowers* by Vincent Van Gogh is one of the world's most famous paintings, and has been reproduced thousands of times. When the original went to auction today, it set a world record price of £24,750,000.

## GERMAN TEENAGER LANDS IN RED SQUARE

**May 28, Moscow** A 19-year-old German boy has flown a light aircraft through Russian air defences and landed it next to the Kremlin in Moscow. Mathias Rust took off from Helsinki, Finland, and flew all the way to the Russian capital. After he landed, Rust signed autographs for passers-by before being arrested by Russian police.

## STORM LASHES BRITAIN

**Oct 16, London** A freak storm swept across southern Britain last night. At times, wind speed reached more than 150 kph (90 mph), well above hurricane force. Hundreds of thousands of buildings were damaged, but few people were hurt. Britain's trees suffered badly; 15 million of them were blown down.

# 1988

## RUSSIAN OCCUPATION OF AFGHANISTAN ENDS

**May 15, Kabul, Afghanistan** The first convoy of Russians soldiers left for home today. A peace treaty was signed last month in Geneva between four nations: Afghanistan, Pakistan, Russia and the USA. The treaty ends the nine-year Russian occupation of Afghanistan. All Russian troops must be out of the country by the end of this year.

Although there is now a ceasefire, the Russians can expect to be attacked by mujahaddin all the way to the border. When the Russians have all gone, the mujahaddin's enemy will be the government troops that defend the main towns. Few people expect the government to survive.

At present there are about 100,000 Russian soldiers and airmen in Afghanistan. There are an unknown number of secret police. During the last nine years, some 13,000 Russian servicemen have been killed on active service here, and a further 35,000 have been wounded.

Mujahaddin carry on the fight in Afghanistan.

## US SHIP SHOOTS DOWN IRANIAN AIRLINER

**July 3, Persian Gulf** In a tragic misunderstanding, an American navy ship, the *Vincennes*, has shot down an Iranian civil airliner. All 290 people on board the airliner were killed.

The *Vincennes* was engaged on a routine patrol of the Persian Gulf to protect neutral shipping from attack by Iranian Silkworm missiles. At the time of the incident, the US ship was involved in a small sea-battle with Iranian patrol boats. Radar operators aboard the *Vincennes* mistook the airliner for an attacking jet fighter in the heat of the battle. An anti-aircraft missile scored a direct hit.

The US government has apologized for the incident, and sent messages of sympathy to the relatives. Even though it was an accident, the loss of the airliner is sure to stir up anti-American feeling in Iran.

## IRAN AND IRAQ STOP FIGHTING

**July 20, Geneva, Switzerland** Both sides in the war between Iran and Iraq have agreed to a ceasefire arranged by the United Nations. This war has cost hundreds of thousands of lives, and has left both countries devastated. The war has been little reported, and most of the fighting has taken place on barren mountains and in deserts. Earlier this year, during the 'war of the cities', civilians were killed during bombardment by long range missiles. Last year, Iraq used mustard gas and nerve gas to stop Iranian attacks. Earlier, they used poison gas to kill those sympathetic to Iran inside Iraq. The other side is no better. The Iranians have sent children as young as 13 to the front line.

# BUSH ELECTED US PRESIDENT

**Nov 8, Washington DC, USA** George Bush, Ronald Reagan's Vice-President, has been elected President of the United States. Bush beat the Democratic contender Michael Dukakis by a significant majority. Dan Quayle is to be the new Vice-President. However, Bush is not as popular as Reagan has been. Less than half those Americans eligible to vote did so, making this the lowest turnout since 1924.

# PAKISTAN HAS WOMAN PREMIER

**Dec 2, Islamabad, Pakistan** Following last month's elections, Benazir Bhutto was today sworn in as Pakistan's first woman Prime Minister. She is the first woman leader of a Muslim country. Ms. Bhutto is the daughter of former president Ali Bhutto, who was overthrown and then executed by President Zia in the 1970s. She takes over from a caretaker government that was installed after President Zia was assassinated in August. She is the leader of the Pakistan People's Party.

# PALESTINIANS RECOGNIZE ISRAEL

**Dec 13, Geneva, Switzerland** At the General Assembly of the United Nations, Yasser Arafat has said that the Palestinians recognize the existence of Israel and renounce terrorism. The General Assembly had to meet in Geneva, because the Americans would not give Arafat a visa to visit New York.

The Palestinian *intifada*, or uprising, in the Israeli-occupied territories is now entering its second year. Arab-owned shops and businesses remain closed, the refugee camps are under strict curfew. Gangs of Palestinian youths continue to taunt Israeli soldiers. So far, 300 Palestinians have been shot dead, and 100 have died of beatings and from exposure to tear gas.

# US AIRLINER BLOWN UP IN MID-AIR

**Dec 21, London**  A bomb has blown up a US airliner over Scotland. All 259 people on board the plane were killed, and wreckage was strewn over a wide area. The flight to New York was packed with people going home for Christmas when it exploded in mid-air. A large piece of the wreckage fell on the Scottish town of Lockerbie, killing 11 local people.

The bomb may be a revenge attack for the shooting down of an Iranian airliner in July.

# CUBAN TROOPS TO QUIT AFRICA

**Dec 22, Geneva, Switzerland**  Representatives from Angola, Cuba and South Africa today signed an agreement that will lead to the independence of Namibia. Under the agreement, Cuban troops will leave Angola. In return, South African troops will leave Namibia.

There are about 50,000 Cuban troops in Angola. Some have been there for more than ten years. Under the agreement, they must go by July 1991.

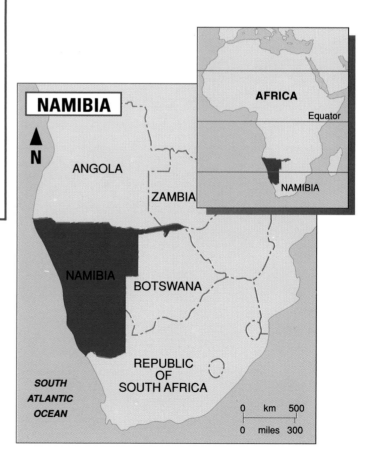

# NEWS IN BRIEF . . .

## NEW YEAR SUPERPOWER GOODWILL

**Jan 1, Washington DC and Moscow** Russia and America were linked by television at the start of the year. For the first time, Russian television showed a five-minute New Year speech from US President Reagan. In return, the US government arranged for American TV companies to show a similar speech by President Gorbachev. Both speeches contained messages of goodwill and hope for the future.

## AUSTRALIAN BICENTENNIAL

**Jan 26, Sydney, Australia** Australia celebrates being 200 years old today. During the festivities a fleet of tall ships is anchoring in Sydney harbour. Sailing ships from all over the world have gathered here to help the nation celebrate.

Not everybody is having a party. A few of the country's Aborigines are using the bicentennial as a platform for protest. They want a much greater say in the development of what was once their land.

## RUSSIAN CHRISTIANS CELEBRATE

**June 5, Moscow** Today the Soviet people celebrated one thousand years of Christianity in their country. The Eastern Orthodox Church was banned throughout the reign of Lenin, Stalin and subsequent hard-line leaders. They imposed atheism on the people as part of the Communist system. However, most people kept their faith alive in secret.

## DRUG BARON SENTENCED

**May 19, Florida, USA** A Colombian drug baron was today sentenced to 'life imprisonment plus 150 years'. He had smuggled three tons of cocaine into the United States. He was one of the leaders of the Medellin cartel, or drug ring, which smuggles much of the cocaine that enters America. He was arrested by the Colombian authorities and sent to the US for trial.

US government anti-drugs policy does much more than give stiff prison sentences to smugglers. During recent months, US troops have been in Bolivia, finding and destroying jungle drug factories.

## EARTHQUAKE IN ARMENIA

**Dec 8, Armenia, southern Russia** A massive earthquake has struck the district of Armenia. An estimated 100,000 people have been killed. Nearly half a million have been made homeless in temperatures below freezing point. President Gorbachev has cut short an overseas visit in order personally to take charge of the relief operation. Several foreign governments have offered to send food,

## NORTH SEA GAS RIG EXPLODES

**July 7, Scotland** An offshore gas platform, Piper Alpha, has exploded and caught fire. At least 160 workers have been killed, and dozens more injured. Emergency services have been fighting the flames through the night, and helicopters are still searching for survivors. It seems the disaster was caused by the failure of a safety valve, which allowed the build-up of flammable gas.

blankets, medical teams and rescue equipment. However, rescue work is difficult because the Armenian countryside is isolated and mountainous.

# 1989

## MASSACRE IN TIAN-AN-MEN SQUARE

**June 4, Beijing, China**    The Chinese authorities have crushed the democracy movement, which was led by students. Between two and five thousand people have been killed during two days of savage repression. Thousands more have been seriously injured. The worst of the violence occurred when soldiers and tanks moved into Tian-an-men Square in the centre of Beijing early this morning. Students' leaders and crowds of their supporters had gathered in the square as a final protest. Many were shot as the soldiers fired at random into the crowds. Others were crushed beneath tanks.

During the last few weeks, it appeared that the movement for democracy was being accepted by China's Communist leadership. However, all hopes of reform have now been wiped out. Deng Xiaoping, China's elderly leader, praised the army for its action against the threat of 'counter-revolutionary agitators'.

## DEMONSTRATORS KILLED IN GEORGIA

**April 9, Georgia, USSR**    Russian internal security troops killed 16 civilian demonstrators early this morning. This is the worst example of state brutality for many years. The incident happened during a demonstration in Tblisi, the capital of the Republic of Georgia.

Earlier, up to 100,000 Georgians had filled the streets, calling for Georgia to become independent. The security troops moved in on a crowd of demonstrators that had surrounded the Town Hall. Most of those killed were women; some were clubbed to death, others were sprayed with poison gas which choked and suffocated them.

Georgia is one of the largest of the 16 republics that make up the USSR. As in most other republics, the native people form a separate ethnic group. Unrest from its ethnic peoples is one of the biggest problems currently facing Russia's leadership. Ethnic unrest could cause Russia to break apart into a number of smaller nations.

## HUNGARY OPENS BORDER

**Sept 12, Budapest, Hungary**    The Hungarian government has relaxed controls over its border with Austria. As a result, thousands of East Germans are crossing over to Western Europe. All summer, East Germans have been gathering in Hungary, hoping to escape. Many have been camping out in the grounds of foreign embassies rather than return home. Hungary's Communist neighbours have loudly criticized the government's action. They claim that Hungary is openly encouraging the move to democracy in other countries.

# SOLIDARITY WINS POLISH ELECTIONS

**June 4, Warsaw, Poland** Solidarity has won all but one of the available seats in the Polish elections. The organization that started out as a trade union has become the country's ruling political party. Poland is the first country in Eastern Europe to elect a non-Communist government. Until April, Solidarity was an illegal organization.

Supporters applaud the news that Solidarity is no longer an illegal organization.

# MASSIVE PRO-DEMOCRACY DEMONSTRATION

**Nov 4, East Berlin** More than 500,000 East Berliners crowded into the city streets tonight. They heard speeches by opponents of the Communist government. This is the largest pro-democracy demonstration so far, and its size is a sign that the government is beginning to lose control. As well as calling for the Berlin Wall to be pulled down, the crowds also shouted for East and West Germany to be re-united.

# BERLIN WALL OPENED

**Nov 10, East Berlin, Germany** East German border guards tonight opened the gates and checkpoints in the Berlin Wall. For the first time in 28 years, Berliners can now pass through freely.

This is the most surprising event so far in a wave of democracy that appears to be sweeping across Eastern Europe. Throughout the summer, Communist governments have been increasingly attacked by the people. There have been massive pro-democracy demonstrations. It looks as though the Iron Curtain is finally being lifted.

# GERMANS FREE TO CROSS BERLIN WALL

**Nov 10, Berlin** "I have stamped other people's passports for four years, and I never thought I would stand on the other side of the counter, I can't believe it." – a border guard.

"When I heard the news I didn't think about a visa, I just got into my car and drove to the border. It was like a dream." – young East German.

"We just wanted to put a foot over the line; we were like children, we just couldn't wait. Our little boy is at home asleep, so we have to go straight back." – East German couple.

"It is breathtaking. All those years I learnt about the anti-fascist protection barrier – it is as if our country has finally opened its eyes to reality." – a history student.

(All quoted in *The Times*)

# DEMOCRATIC PRESIDENT FOR CZECHOSLOVAKIA

**Dec 29, Prague, Czechoslovakia** The playwright Vaclav Havel has been elected the new President of Czechoslovakia. He was the unanimous choice of the country's new Popular Assembly. Havel is Czechoslovakia's first non-Communist head of state since 1948.

The Popular Assembly has also appointed Alexander Dubček as its first Chairman. Dubček tried to liberalize Czech politics during the 'Prague Spring' of 1968. His efforts were crushed by a Russian invasion. Although Communists still have many top jobs, their power is rapidly declining. The new focus of Czech politics is 'Civic Forum', an alliance of the old opposition groups.

# ANC LEADER RELEASED

**Oct 15, Pretoria, South Africa** The winds of change are blowing in South Africa. Today, the government released eight political prisoners, including Walter Sisulu, a leading member of the African National Congress (ANC). Sisulu has been imprisoned since 1964, when he was jailed with Nelson Mandela. Announcing the release, President de Klerk stated that the ANC would remain a banned organization. Mr. de Klerk refused to say whether Nelson Mandela will also be released soon.

# REVOLUTION IN ROMANIA

**Dec 25, Sofia, Romania** After three days of bitter street fighting, Romania's Communist government has been overthrown. Its hated dictator, President Ceausescu, is dead. An alliance of soldiers and citizens has defeated the Securitate, the secret police who remained loyal to the President.

Weeks of unrest broke into open revolution on December 22, when crowds began booing a speech by the President. Within minutes, the crowd's mood had turned ugly. Ceausescu escaped from the presidential palace by helicopter. He was soon captured, and after a court martial, he and his wife were executed by firing squad. Tonight, the streets of Sofia still ring with gunfire, as police and the army hunt the last few Securitate men.

President Nicolai Ceausescu and his wife Elena are shown on television during their trial.

# 1989

# NEWS IN BRIEF . . .

## CRACK MENACE CROSSES ATLANTIC

**July 31, London** European police chiefs have been alerted to the menace of the highly dangerous drug 'crack'. In the United States, crack-smoking has become the greatest social problem in most large cities.

Crack is a potent form of cocaine that can be smoked in a special pipe. Users often become violent and confused, but the major problem is that crack is highly addictive. Thousands of American teenagers have already become crack addicts.

## AUTHOR IN HIDING

**Feb 14, London** British author Salman Rushdie has gone into hiding after threats on his life. The threats follow the publication of his new book *The Satanic Verses*. Islamic scholars claim that the book is deeply insulting to all Muslims. In Tehran, the Ayatollah Khomeini has condemned Rushdie, and has called for all true Muslims to try and kill him. The British government has protested to Iran.

## SHAKESPEARE'S THEATRE FOUND

**Oct 12, London** Archaeologists working on a building site have found the remains of the Globe Theatre. It was here that many of Shakespeare's plays were first performed. Building work has been halted while experts look at the remains.

The Globe Theatre was circular in shape, and made almost entirely out of wood. All that now remains is part of the foundations.

## SAN FRANCISCO EARTHQUAKE

**Oct 18, San Francisco, USA** A powerful earthquake shook this California city today. More than 250 people were killed, and hundreds more were injured. The 15-second quake brought down a stretch of elevated highway. Many of the dead and injured were trapped in their cars when the earthquake struck. The city lies on a geological fault.

A businessman walks to work through rubble in San Francisco.

## SINGLE CURRENCY FOR EUROPE

**December 30, Brussels** The European Economic Community has agreed in principle to an economic and monetary union. This means that all member states will one day use the same currency. Some countries, such as Britain, are not happy with the decision. They see monetary union as the first step towards a single European state. Their sense of national identity rejects the idea of a unified Europe. Those who support it say it would help trade between member countries.

## COMPENSATION FOR AUSTRALIAN SOLDIERS

**Sept 4, Sydney, Australia** The Australian government has agreed to pay compensation to a number of Australian servicemen. After taking part in British H-bomb tests during the 1950s, the men suffered from the effects of exposure to atomic radiation. Many more than would normally do so developed blood and bone cancer. The decision taken here in Australia will encourage British ex-servicemen who are hoping for compensation for similar injuries sustained at work.

# PEOPLE OF THE EIGHTIES

## Ronald Reagan (b. 1911)

After a successful career as a film actor, Reagan turned to politics. During 1967-75 he served as Governor of California, the biggest state in America. He was elected President in 1980; people liked his tough, rather old-fashioned views. Under his leadership, military spending increased, and foreign policy was more aggressive. During his second four-year term in office, Reagan was involved in the 'Irangate' scandal. He retired in 1988.

## Margaret Thatcher (b. 1925)

Mrs. Thatcher served as a minister in the Conservative government before being elected party leader in 1975. After she became Prime Minister in 1979, Mrs. Thatcher's tough financial policies soon brought inflation under control and revived the economy. In world affairs she was a strong leader, and earned international respect.

Under Margaret Thatcher's leadership many people became richer, but a new 'underclass' of poor people also grew.

## Ayatollah Ruhollah Khomeini (1900-89)

Iranian religious and political leader. Khomeini was trained as an Islamic scholar, and exiled from Iran by the Shah in 1964. In 1979, he returned to Iran to lead the Islamic Revolution. Under his rule, Iran returned to a repressive system of religious law. Women, for instance, were forbidden to uncover their heads in public. In foreign policy, Khomeini was bitterly opposed both to the capitalist United States, and to atheist Russia.

## Nelson Mandela (b. 1918)

Black South African leader. Mandela has been a member of the African National Congress (ANC) since 1943. He was a supporter of the idea of an armed struggle against the apartheid regime of South Africa. In 1964, Mandela was arrested, tried for treason, and sentenced to life imprisonment. At various times during the 1970s and 1980s, people around the world campaigned for his release. The South African authorities refused to consider giving Mandela his freedom until he renounced the use of violence. He was freed in 1990, and was made leader of the ANC.

# Yasser Arafat (b. 1929)

Palestinian leader. Arafat first became involved in Palestinian politics in 1954, when he co-founded the Al Fatah guerrilla group. In 1969, he became chairman of the Palestine Liberation Organization (PLO). Since 1973, he has gradually reduced military action against Israel, and has emphasized diplomacy instead. In 1988, Arafat renounced terrorism, and stated that the PLO recognized the existence of Israel.

# Lech Walesa (b. 1943)

Polish political leader. Walesa first became involved in politics during a shipyard strike in 1980. His unofficial movement grew into the Solidarity trade union. In 1983, Walesa was awarded the Nobel Peace Prize for the non-violence of his campaign. In 1989 he was elected as a non-Communist MP in the Polish parliament, and as President in 1990.

# Mikhail Gorbachev (b. 1931)

Russian leader. Gorbachev became a member of the Russian Politburo in 1980, and in 1985 he succeeded Chernenko as General Secretary. Gorbachev has tried to reform Russia with his ideas of *glasnost* (openness), and *perestroika* (reconstruction). He tried to tackle Russia's severe economic problems. Gorbachev has also faced the problems of ethnic and nationalist unrest inside Russia. During his leadership, Communist rule collapsed in Eastern Europe.

# Bob Geldof (b. 1955)

Irish musician and charity fundraiser. Geldof rose to fame during the 1970s with a group called the Boomtown Rats. When he saw pictures of the 1984 famine in Ethiopia, he immediately wanted to help. Working with others in the music industry, Geldof organized the Band Aid record 'Do They Know It's Christmas?' in 1984, and the Live Aid concerts in 1985. Through his efforts, tens of millions of pounds were raised for famine relief.

# For the first time ever

| 1980 | UK/Canada | First international public facsimile (fax) |
| | Japan/Holland | Compact laser discs go on sale |
| | USA | First medical use of genetic engineering on human patients |
| **1981** | UK | First true 'pocket television' developed |
| | USA | Hologram video game goes on sale |
| | | Vaccine against serum hepatitis approved |
| **1982** | Japan | Prototype magnetic disc camera on display |
| | USA | Super-computer performs 100 million operations per second |
| | | Boeing 757 takes first test flight |
| **1983** | UK | Biodegradable plastic developed |
| | | Maglev train (magnetic levitation linear propulsion passenger car) carries first passengers |
| | USA | Superconducting transistor developed |
| **1984** | USA | 1 million bit memory computer chip developed |
| | | Holograms placed on credit cards |
| | Japan | Computer translates 60,000 words per minute (translation from Japanese to English) |
| **1985** | Japan | Video camera using 8mm tape goes on sale |
| | | Artificial tooth root invented |
| | USA/ Switzerland | Scanning tunnelling microscope invented |
| | UK | Solar-powered pay phones developed |

| 1986 | Japan | Electronic 'drumless' drumsticks go on sale |
| | West Germany | Gall stones treated with miniature lasers |
| **1987** | USA | Genetically altered bacteria released into the environment (to prevent crop frost damage) |
| | Japan | Prototype 16 million bit memory computer chip announced |
| | Japan/Holland | Compact video disc players go on sale |
| **1988** | USA | V-22 tilt-rotor aircraft makes test flight |
| | | B-2 Stealth bomber makes first flight |
| | | CD singles go on sale |
| | Japan | Video 'Walkman' reaches the shops |
| **1989** | USA | Miniature heart pump installed in patient for first time |
| | France | 'Transparent' X-Ray table invented |
| | West Germany | Chainsaw fitted with a catalytic converter goes on sale |

# New words and expressions

The following words and expressions came into popular use during the Eighties. Do you know what they all mean?

acid-house party
cell-phone
cellulite
CD
Contra
deconstructivism
desktop publishing
Dinkie (Dual Income – No Kids)
E-number
environmentally friendly
filofax (TM)
footsie
genetic fingerprint

green politics
hiphop
networking
post-modern
power dressing
rap music
Red Nose Day
sampling
shellsuit
snow-wash
Sports Aid
stealth technology
user friendly
yomping

# Glossary

**apartheid**: system of legalized racism in South Africa. Under apartheid, non-white people do not have the vote and are subject to a number of repressive and humiliating laws.

**cartel**: group of manufacturers who arrange to control the price of goods in the shops.

**cruise missile**: small medium-range guided missile that can be very accurate. It can carry either a nuclear or conventional warhead.

**dormant**: sleeping, inactive.

**fundamentalism**: branch of a religion that has a 'back to basics' approach. Believers often insist on the literal meaning of sacred texts.

**Iron Curtain**: name for the border which existed between Western Europe and the Communist countries of Eastern Europe.

**KGB**: branch of the Russian government responsible for internal security, border guards and foreign intelligence (spying).

**militia**: group of armed civilians. Some are well-intentioned and well-disciplined, others are little more than gangsters.

**mujahaddin**: Afghan Muslim guerrillas who fought against the Russian invaders and the Communist government of Afghanistan.

**NATO**: North Atlantic Treaty Organization; a military alliance that includes the United States and most of Western Europe.

**Politburo**: the inner cabinet that governs Russia and establishes policy.

**public spending**: money that a government spends, providing services for its citizens.

**Shiite**: belonging to a minority branch of the Muslim religion. Most Shiites live in Iran.

**star wars**: system of satellite-mounted anti-missile defences developed in the United States. Otherwise known as the Strategic Defence Initiative.

**Warsaw Pact**: the military alliance between Russian and the Communist countries of Eastern Europe.

# Further reading

*The Eighties*: Edward Grey. Wayland 1989

*The Middle East since 1945*: Heather Blaney and Richard Lawless. Batsford 1989

*The Revolution in Iran*: Akbar Husain. Wayland 1986

*Arab-Israeli Wars*: Ken Hills. Cherrytree Press 1991

*Glasnost: The Gorbachev Revolution*: Elizabeth Roberts. Hamish Hamilton 1989